AGAIN
THE RED FOX

Franco Pagnucci

Water's Edge Press
Tucson, AZ

This collection of poems is a work of imagination.

Again The Red Fox © Franco Pagnucci, 2024
All rights reserved.

ISBN: 978-1-952526-18-3
Library of Congress Control Number: 2023948592

Published in the United States

Water's Edge Press LLC
Tucson, Arizona

Credits:
Excerpt from *Extremely Loud & Incredibly Close*
used with permission from Jonathan Safran Foer.
Data for "Monarch 433" taken from MonarchWatch.org
Cover image licensed through iStock.com
Cover and book design by Water's Edge Press LLC

"Pagnucci's intention is 'to give you what I saw,' to illuminate specific moments of connection with the natural world that show the ordinary in a new way. His reflections on these connections cast a new light on our own world—and ourselves. An enjoyable and insightful read."

—William K. Spofford, Ph.D, Emeritus Professor UW-P, Study Abroad

"*Again the Red Fox* is a real winner. I adore the brevity of inspired moments—not easy to do while capturing the solidity of the real, allowing the reader to imagine and celebrate and wonder."

—Claire Dulgar, former English teacher, Anoka-Hennepin District, Minneapolis

"*Again the Red Fox* is an amazing collection of poems by Franco Pagnucci that takes readers on an incredible journey through nature. Though the poet shows us many of earth's creatures, it's the presence of the red fox—who appears with dignity and quiet strength in magical moments— that reminds us of our own mortality. Bravo! And thank you!"

—Geri Bates, former Nurse

"Those who value the rustic, sylvan charms of country living will find themselves well-met with Franco Pagnucci's *Again the Red Fox*. He observes and records the ancient and ongoing drama of life on earth with clarity, tenderness, and truth. 'How easy to forget oneself/here where one counts for nothing.'"

—Kristine Lendved, Director, Forest Lodge Library,
Cable/Namakagon, Wisconsin

"Pagnucci is a wordsmith who can capture an event of nature, no matter how momentary, and put it into beautiful words. He does this especially with the *Fabled Fox*, who is the red fox that dances through many of his poems. The fox is fleeting, only seen so briefly, then Franco's poetic imagination takes over."

—Rev. Charles Reichenbacher, OSB, Priest-Monk of Marmion Abbey, Aurora, Illinois

"*Again the Red Fox* calls the objects of its desire with soft sounds and subtle songs; this must be how you talk to foxes and lovers so they'll step their fleet feet into your poetry and your world."

—Jessi Waugh, former science teacher. Yoga instructor, poet/writer

"Franco Pagnucci's new book feels like a shared collection of cherished photos. *Again the Red Fox* is a beautiful book that, at the end, reminds us of that moment when we realize summer is over, 'the hummingbirds are gone,' the red fox has entered the den, and we are left longing for more."

—Lorraine Francioni, former language arts teacher

"Franco Pagnucci's latest book of poetry is a true pleasure. He transports us to a calm place of reflection, as though we sit next to him, taking in tranquil nature, familiar images painted so clearly. Pagnucci's poems bring peace and are an eloquent reminder to take a moment and be present."

—Kate Tilman, MD

Books by Franco Pagnucci

Firstborn (North Star Press, 2016)
Breath of the Onion: Italian-American Anecdotes (North Star Press, 2015)
Tracks on Damp Sand (North Star Press, 2014)
Ancient Moves (Bur Oak Press, 1998)
I Never Had a Pet (Bur Oak Press, 1992)
Out Harmsen's Way (Fireweed Press, 1991)

Anthologies Edited by Franco Pagnucci

New Roads Old Towns (A Rountree Publication, UW-Platteville, 1988)
Face the Poem (Bur Oak Press, 1979)

To the 1001 Book Group—

special, creative, interesting friends,
who fostered the best in all of us:

Virginia,
Angelo,
Mary,
Jim,
Deb,
Lynn,
Frank,
Claire,
Abett,
Ron,
Sylvia,
George (in memoriam),
Susan (my wife).

Before the Late Spring Rains

Before the Late Spring Rains 1
Andrew Wyeth's *Night Sleeper* 2
Dusk or Soon After 3
Juices Gone 4
Fabled Fox 5
The Lid 6
Kingbird 7
The Creek 8
Say Those Words 9
You Could Smell the Wind 10
Bobbing Heads 11
Declawed Cat 12
Dawdling 13
Wings 14
Waiting 15
Morning 16
Bass 17
The Beaver 18
Still Life: Mid-July 19
River Otter 20
The Red Fox Again 21
For Mother 22
Once a Common Loon Flying Over 23
A Yard Full of Smudgy-white Geese 24
When Watermelons Had Seeds 25
Sunday Evening. Rain 26
The Place 27

Where you were headed

Where You Were Headed ... 31
Sails ... 32
Honeygar ... 33
Smile and Let Go ... 34
Give Me Patience! Mamma Would Have Said ... 35
You Saw That Fox Running ... 36
Blooms of Late August ... 37
Dive-Dapper ... 38
Sometimes You Push Back the Curtains ... 39
Monarch 433 ... 40
Wind ... 41
September Sky ... 42
In Hot, Windless, Late September ... 43
Uncle ... 44
The Cadillac Drawing ... 45
Clarinet Sonata on MPR ... 46
Only Gulls Here ... 47
Hummingbirds Gone ... 48
In Late Afternoon ... 49
Big Bluestem ... 50
Blackbirds ... 51
Deep Cut ... 52
First Snow ... 53
Monday Afternoon ... 54
Two Plump Brown-Speckled Grouse ... 55
Nine Mallards ... 56
They Woke Me on a Winter Morning ... 57

What I See And Remember

What I See and Remember 61
Solitary Prints 62
da Vinci's *Lady with Ermine* 63
Flowers Live Awhile 64
Tundra Swans 65
Running on Snow Crust 66
Pine Grosbeak 67
The Fawn 68
Peepers 69
The Finale 70
Crossing Point 71
That Day 72
In the Night 73
How a Small Deer 74
Fishy Words 75
Birds Come in Bunches 76
House Wren 77
Indigo Bunting 78
Line Tension 79
Towhee Along Kelly Lake Road 80
Late Snapper 81
Mid-June the Muskrat 82
All Day You Were Gone 83
Cranes 84
Gnats 85
Loon Moment 86
Come Late 87
The Hatchlings 88
Walking in the Distance 89

Walking Into The Poem

I write because I want to give you what I saw. Maybe what I saw wasn't unusual, but the way the light hit or the way what I saw was turned or how it shifted in the light caught my eye. And at that moment I would have thought you, *there*, to see what I saw. Maybe we wouldn't have talked. At least we would have nodded as we walked away, each of us remembering that moment's light on what we saw.

Franco Pagnucci, Cedar Point, NC 2023

BEFORE THE LATE SPRING RAINS

Before the Late Spring Rains

Early. Gray-dark, heavy morning.

She stood in the middle of the road.
You could tell she'd been looking at us.

I said, *The fox*, and pointed, but she was gone.

Andrew Wyeth's *Night Sleeper*

He said the dog meant to be anyone's
seemed like someone else's dog that night.

It was the laundry bag by her sleeping head below the window.
It was the worry of the full bag under the open window
that never slept that night
while the moon rose higher and went out the other window
and on over the mill
and even over *Papà's* mill,
now only a few piles of rubble
under the shadowed brambles of the deep ravine in the hazy hills above Pisa.

It was the moon going on through the dark night alone.

Dusk or Soon After

Peepers suddenly stopped calling,
and I knew something must be wrong.

When they started up again,
the sound came from another room
at the far end of the river channel to Birch.

Their muted calls saddened me, then.
You'd left in mid-afternoon,

and I heard a diminished world.

Juices Gone

The nestling was a few
blue-gray feathers flattened on the sun-hot asphalt.

As evening darkened,
the feathers' blue-touch disappeared.
A hot asphalt smell hung over the road.

In the road swales, blueberries were fat and warm with sun.

Fabled Fox

If she doesn't live in our neighborhood,
at least we inhabit the circle of her range.

At times she'll strut across our paths,
sometimes stepping into the road to pose and look at us,
then leap into the shade of woods
before we get near.

She's like an aching wish that fills you,
a choice piece of furniture you've never found.

Her tail floats behind her, black-banded, white-tipped.

The Lid

Tonight, a dark high sky
and below it clouds darker still, spreading.
Only a few sprinkles fall.
Then a circle of light opens in a corner,
a boatful of light,
blue sky and sun ride the water alongside the canoe
and over the clear shallow bottom of the river channel.
How easy to forget oneself
here where one counts for nothing.
Wind riffles the lake.
The lid of the sky closes again.
A pale light from that corner spreads halfway across the lake.

Kingbird

The kingbird twittered in the May air,
and when he landed in the oak top
still twittering to himself,
his white chest against the green
was like the hawthorn in the dawn.
The blue of evening got a little bluer.
The earth's spin felt a little slower.

The Creek

Some places it drops
the sound inside a hollow log.
Some places it rushes through green grasses and old leaves,
tinkling spoons on thick glass.
Where it slithers over moss,
silence spreads onto gray-white sleeping slugs
waiting under stagnant backwater pools and a water-logged elm,
the creek's soft touch encircling and hauling their sleeping sounds ...
You find your breathing pacing its long, slow runs.

Say Those Words

Brown was the color
of my true love's hair
and the color of her furry coat.
How often old thoughts
return there though March winds
blew snow-dust across a brown, hard prairie.
But say those words,
hesitant as an early April,
and from wet snow rise crocus, squills, daffodils.

You Could Smell the Wind

and the morning when the red fox stopped and pointed her nose.
Her ears caught sounds where they started.

Her paws paused. Her eyes
flared. A creature flattened along an edge.

Bobbing Heads

A bird with white undersides
circled and banked along high clouds,
then dove like a missile ...
You, half-blind without your glasses, thought it was a seagull
when it suddenly pulled out of full dive
and rose—a loud whistle, an osprey over the treetops,
and we understood how easily, regretful endings happen.

Declawed Cat

He looked from the rocker seat to the headrest,
moved closer, left paw lifted,
saw the effort it would take, through to the leap.

We understood.
Each afternoon we had contemplated the jump
from the gravel pile across the two-foot ditch
and up to our concrete wall lookout.

Once after a dare, skinny John Anthony missed the top hold of the wall.
The tip of a tie rod sticking out gashed his chest as he slid

down. He didn't cry. Lifting his bloody
T-shirt, he looked down at the scratched,
flayed skin from left of his right nipple
to his belly button.

He crumpled into the ditch below us—
a deflated balloon.

You shouldn't have dared me, he said.

Dawdling

Seventeen wild turkeys
pecking in a fall afternoon
down a steep embankment.

An old one stood
like a watch tower
slowly stepping after them.

They pecked in the sun
without looking up.
Wind rose off the highway.

You could feel the old one's
heavy arm draped on them,
and holding us firm

in our shell of metal and glass,
we grownups wishing
to dawdle in the sun of that hillside.

Wings

Say you're a tree swallow,
a small bird the size of a sparrow,
and a raven-sized crow stalks your place.
You can't put him off. You have a nest.
From a broken-top maple you dive
onto his back as he hops to a stump.

I was a fifth grader when a sixth grader
sat in front of me. Maybe I tapped his back,
said something or asked a silly question.
He turned and jabbed a sharpened pencil
in my forearm. I said, *Hey!* He turned
and jabbed again. That's how my fall went.

Next day I waited on the playground. Jumped
from behind a tree and had him by the ribs.
He dropped and topped me to the ground.
He'd failed fifth and outweighed me.
He lived on Dean by Moline Malibu Ironworks.
Uncle Ivo put in 20 years. Never took a sick day.
Retired to the Old Country but didn't stay.

Waiting

Waiting for us to drive past, the red fox
held a mouthful. Maybe a rib with meat shreds
she'd found and was carrying to a secret place.
You've imagined a taste for so long,
your mouth hangs open. Warmth oozes
around your tongue, but you don't swallow.
Could be heading to meet the one
who sometimes makes you forget to breathe.

Morning

On the wet wood of the walkway
a small toad the color of dry dirt,
quiet as a dust ball.
I remembered
a night breath
from you.

Bass

A bass fingerling came up and side-mouth snatched
a white moth, airy as a Mayfly.
Held it.
Maybe another from the same school felt the lurch,
saw a flash of light overhead,
leapt up and grazed the one's lip.
Missed the moth.
The lucky one tightened jaw,
fishtailed,
and disappeared as the gaping-mouth other
completing a backward arc,
splashed.
The lake closed spreading calmness outward.

The Beaver

Long before we reached the bend of the river channel,
the beaver must have been there exploring
in the dim light and shadow of trees.
He slapped his flat tail on the water
with a cannonball's *thunk*.
Our insides leaped.
Our canoe rose and wobbled
riding the edges of his waves—
we two frogs set adrift.

Still Life: Mid-July

When we stopped at Mamma's and Papà's
while they were in Tuscany,
I found a short gray unbroken ash-skin
in the gray silence on the cellar floor,
the cap on the wall hook,
his slippers side by side
at the foot of the stairs.

A house with no people ...
I no go look,
Uncle Ivo said when I handed back the keys.
How garden?

Eh ... I shrugged.

His right hand waved it all away.

River Otter

Then the otter that came up
above water with a fish in his mouth
swam under the dock
and under the clump of alder brush
hanging over the lake.

You would have loved
the smacking his mouth and tongue made on the bluegill
as he swallowed and swam out
from under the brush
and up shore on his back.

The Red Fox Again

Driving back after ten, we see the red fox
cross where County A curves and begins its climb.
Suddenly sitting next to me you enter the poem
as if I'd said *I'm leaving you*.

Smaller, less pure red than I remember
a fox, this one in the headlights has buff
on the back and tail, but the tail is huge,
bigger than the animal and, as they say, floating.

The other, seven years before, crossing on the curve
looked back at me over a shoulder like the friend whose funeral I'd missed.

I see our lives together
strung in small beads of bright light. All the years
like nothing else about the dull day but that fox coming across,
looking at me like the sunset of the flagship going over the horizon.

Pinpoints of light splayed against our lives.
Harold shoots himself at seventy-six for a burden we never knew.
Light plays the world for us like that,
holds up a square where the entering bullet burns and lets go.

The light burning and letting go,
our lives on the curve where the red fox
climbs or falls toward the dark valley of the Little Platte.

For Mother

Almost ninety-five,
to her *then* and *now*
are in flux,

and we flow where a grebe
marks places on the lake—
down for a count of twelve,
up for one, two, three.

He is still back in the marsh of the lake
while a kingfisher rattles past
and plunks into the water beyond the dock
like a mallet-to-gong.

Once a Common Loon Flying Over

Birch Lake Road wailed … and wailed
again … A fingerling dangled from his bill.
The extra wails, a little strained,

out of a mouth holding a dangling fish.
You know how a fish will squirm
and fishtail feeling a loosened hold.

Still, don't believe that that loon
was showing off or being loud
as crows get louder over anything.

The common loon was
wailing to remind the waiting
one below that he was coming home.

A Yard Full of Smudgy-white Geese

Although we can imagine a story
in which a boy foolish enough
to believe what we dream up
picks up his pen one moonless night ...

the geese don't leave
for some uncharted northern lake.
The afternoon dims. Maybe a storm approaches.
The geese waddle off, some dragging sagging bottoms
toward the trough piled with green pellets.

When Watermelons Had Seeds

The red fox was leaping
and swatting at wheat-colored moths.

Maybe a game in slant morning light
like spitting black watermelon seeds off a porch.

Whenever she pawed a moth out of the air,
she sat on her red haunches

in dry buff grass under the red stop sign,
smacking and smacking her brown lips.

Sunday Evening. Rain

Looking back,
I saw the one-year-old—
her spot of red in the air.
You stood at the gate,
waving into a blur.

Don't look back, I said to the two boys.

Make a U-turn! Make a U-turn!
The nine-year-old said again. *Make a U-turn!*

Seven hours north,
I still felt the urge
but never said.

The Place

Too far to hear what they're saying,
you figure the two are after walleye ...
The old one in gray jacket casts a huge red plug,
watches the boat bob toward the shore.
A boatful of wind brings them closer.

We'd be happy with a few blue gills,
he says in your direction. *Where's a good spot?*

The one in the yellow rain suit
switches from red and white spoon
to leaderless hook and nightcrawler.
In case no walleye passes, he'll troll for gills.
He puts on his yellow rain cap and mans the Mercury outboard.

The place to where you pointed from the dock,
at heart never changes—there or a little farther up
beyond that channel, just short of the horizon.
I haven't been here in years,
the one in gray says.

The wind kicks up gusts of fine June rain.

WHERE YOU WERE HEADED

Where You Were Headed

It didn't matter.

It was how the pileated woodpecker
squatted to her belly
and draped and dipped her neck,
one side,

then the other,
to her chest
in a rivulet of melted snow.
It was how the wind

rubbed across the pines
and the clear melt
washed down every road rut
all that afternoon.

Sails

You never hold back anything,
not even a thought of yourself.
While I, I remember the bent
wire earrings as my gift.
How they hung from your lobes
like sails. If I close my eyes,
I find I can float in your selfless sea.

Honeygar

Spouting on about a poem
saving a moment for tomorrow
and tomorrows, I was Pooh Bear,
elevating the prime ingredient in the mix
of cider vinegar, honey, and water
I was drinking.
You sat bouncing
on your white body ball,
hip joints undulating like Tigger's,
and saying, *Honey? Gar? Honey-
garrrrrrrrrrrrrr?* in the mirror of your inner walls.

Smile and Let Go

Remembering the warm fragrance, I was suddenly there
and heard the horseshoes and the rims of the wagon wheels
echoing off the stones below our windows,
the fruit and vegetable vendor's voice chanting:
Cocomeri! Cocomeri! Dolci! Dolci! Qui! Cocomeri!
Watermelons! Watermelons! Sweet !Sweet! Here! Watermelons!

I looked out, then ran down the stairs to a watermelon
fragrant piazza. Papà was already by the stopped wagon load
of watermelons. The old vendor with the warn, brown felt hat
sat on the wagon's wooden bench and cradled in his lap two halves

of a round, dark, dark green watermelon from whose center
he had cut and extracted on the tip of his old, pointed knife
a one-inch square, four-inch-long wedge and was extending it out
to Pierangelo, the postmaster's son, who stood in front of Papà,
Papà who now must have been trying to smile and let go as we watched
Pierangelo slide the chunk off the knife and raise it over his open mouth.

Give Me Patience! Mamma Would Have Said

Four turkeys stood at the side
of the highway, watching us
come out of the curve and up the hill.
You slowed and stopped the car as if
you had come to a CROSSWALK sign.

One of the turkeys understood
because she started into a walk,
crossing just then. Two others followed
her lead in a beeline behind her,
like freight cars of a slow-moving train.

Only the fourth, flustered
with an armful of thoughts swirling,
dashed headlong down the swale
like the man repeating and repeating himself,
never hearing anything you said.

You Saw That Fox Running

You came into the room,
and we took half a turn
to a Neil Young song,
and I played my harmonica
in your ear. Why should it
now remind me of the red fox
in her half-black phase,
running across the road
and disappearing into the woods?
You said how you'd waited all day.

Blooms of Late August

After a chill night,
a morning thick with fog,
a scummy lake,
and warblers rushing through,
the day warmed with promise.

Then in the dusk,
on the curve of the river channel
air bubbles popping through a veil
of late blooms and a foot below,
we saw the ancient snapper,
the color of black silt and as thick as a life vest,
pass and disappear into the quickening darkness.

Dive-Dapper

That grebe,
that brown water bird,
dive-dapper, helldiver
to some, is gone,

and the lake
feels diminished.
Maybe only you
looking out a window
and I know he was here.

In late September,
in late afternoon we saw him
making a fisherman's pass
and dive east to west
out where the reeds start.

A fair northwest wind blew in,
pulled yellow leaves off the birch.

Sometimes You Push Back the Curtains

and find the red fox
standing on a stump.

She looks at you,
and you know
summer has slipped by

and the years.
Your mother's age marks
are on the back of your hands.

The fox looks mottled
in her new gray with black spots.

Monarch 433

> Tagged in Maquoketa, Iowa, "Sep. 7, 2014"
> Recovered in Michoacon, Mexico, "Feb 3, 2015"

Humbling to think he travelled 2000
miles without eating. Each new wind,

its damp or biting edge, its straw-raw dryness
must have shaken his flight and the longing
for sun on a grassy green sidehill

he couldn't imagine. He knew sun. Sun
had warmed him when he crawled out the shuck
and unfolded damp wings at the top of the split back.

We imagine that from what we know.
He had to let go to light and wind all his desires.

Wind

Love the wind when it's reckless
and wild. After heavy rain,
the lake whooshes the shore.
Yellow leaves fly off the birch. *Goodbye!*

Goodbye! Spread your arms and sail.
Let the summery gusts take you.

That edge of coldness ...
That darkening sky in the northwest ...
It's done it all day. Hang with the wind.
Reckless and wild, it can change direction.

September Sky

In September the sky has a cold blue.
The alder and willow brush,
the reeds and ferns and grasses
along the shore show brown tips and edges,

and I cling to you, my love,
as if the changing angle of the light
was something new and unexpected.

We know the old routine.
We're older and see the sham of leaders,
systems, and tradition.
Even our old desires have lost heat.

Things look clearer in September light.
The two flag-flying fishermen
urinating in the lake seem all wrong.

In Hot, Windless, Late September

When we see bluebirds on the wires above the road
and passing robins
turning curled leaves and ferns along the swales,

even if we've missed the eagle's fall flirtatious rushes
or if we forgot to look out or if we didn't notice anything at all,
we'll find that April never waited.

Uncle

> "Time was passing like a hand waving
> from a train window I wanted to be on."
> Jonathan Safran Foer, from *Extremely Loud & Incredibly Close*

The huge oval boulder I straddled shook and shifted
when the evening commuter with three passenger cars whizzed by.
In front of me, the small dead willow alongside the creek still trembled
a little even after the train had disappeared into the evening glow.

Uncle sat on the grassy slope of the embankment by a flaming sumac,
where the boulders ended a hundred feet down track.
We waited for doves that usually came for a drink before dark.

Back in the car, Uncle Jerry said, *Not like last season!*
I need to close my eyes a minute before we head back.
He lowered his head to the side of the headrest and slept.

I watched him sleep and thought about Uncle Jerry,
the hunter of birds on the wing and how he loved a cold slice
of watermelon and a crusty bread with a spread of soft, blue cheese,
and I thought of how easily he let go and fell asleep.

The Cadillac Drawing

I stood with Annie,
blonde and uninterested in cars.
She had the Cadillac's pink
along her neck, under her hair,
and in the skin holding her eyes. She held
onto my arm, and from the far side of the booth
we circled the prize once, twice, and a third time,
she whispering in my ear
about nothing I can remember. The scent of her lipstick
sticks in my mind like the pink of that car
I saw Elvis photographed in once—
the sky blue, the car's pink glittering
like sunny water, wind in the hair of Elvis's passenger.

If we'd heard that the King couldn't play
guitar and only pretended, we could let it go
when we heard he was taking lessons trying to learn.

Clarinet Sonata on MPR

Highway 27 north, late afternoon,
43°, rain. Maybe it felt like snow.
October started colder. Old injuries
echoed snow forecast along the North

Shore. But when you looked right or
left, all the colors there were spreading
deeper into woods, even into rainy dark.
The earth was flaming red, orange,
yellow, green and was reaching up.

Only Gulls Here

Wind brought them,
squawking with hunger.
They circled and banked,
dropped on cool glitters of white,
on breaking bubbles of water.

From the far ends of the lake
the two came together
and floated on the water
like an old couple rocking.

Hummingbirds Gone

Wind gusts of snow
nudged at the house.
Windows in their frames
luffed like loose sails.
Wall corners strained and creaked
against each other like the sides of a ship
under gloomy skies of November.

Still, we didn't worry.
The potted cactus looking south
was a bouquet of hovering hummingbirds,
and the snipped basil bushed out thick and green.

In Late Afternoon

Some days you look up,
longing to count the stars,
but other times you think
even the sky must envy
our lake in late afternoons
when a flock of small ducks
in tight, dark coats stops.
How they waggle and stretch upward
and sit back though cold falls fast.

Big Bluestem

And a red fox loped across the road in front of our car
and stopped to watch us from a field of tall grass
where an old man's shack once stood.
This year no one mentioned the old tin bucket
hung and waiting from a nail the old man
must have driven in the tree.
Wind swayed the clumps of big bluestem
that had come back to that field
where the diamond-shaped head of the fox stopped
and turned to look at us over a shoulder
from the place she parted in the tall, tall grass.

Blackbirds

Inlets along St. Louis Bay
are full of gulls and ducks and geese.
The slip-docks are drying out along the shore.
Yachts and sailboats,
some in a daze of blue plastic,
nap farther back.

Seeing the dry summer fallen
on itself and already forgotten,
we're glad for another gray
November afternoon.
All the blackbirds gone,
crows dawdle and crisscross happily.

Deep Cut

Amazing how the cut sealed
and healed from the inside
outward toward the surface.

Then the thumb bent again,
not a full bend and still stiffly,
but today the feel
was a remembered nobility.

The two creases visible in new
red skin bent without fear of tearing,
blood coursing like spring sap
to the nail and thumb tip,

though only a few leaves were left
on the trees that early November.

First Snow

Large, huge flakes fell
with a rush,
though it was early morning,
early November,
and a great flock of small dark ducks
splashed down on the lake,
then paddled in circles and dove,
feeding and dawdling,
as we did those days
when we had all the warm time in our hands.

Monday Afternoon

The interstate heading south
is a rush of hunters in trucks
hauling dead deer.

It's fifty degrees,
foggy. I'd worry
about spoiling the meat,
but the drivers
that pass us
look satisfied.
No matter what,
tonight, they'll hang
their meat from a tree or swing posts
at the side of the house.

Some have bumper stickers—
Support Our Troops.

Two Plump Brown-Speckled Grouse

They bob along, bobbing,
spindly branches
of the ironwood trees

plucking brown-husked,
sleeping buds to branch ends.
They hop and flutter to other
branches, eating everything.

We wish the cold wind blowing
would shake and give
them pause to think.

Nine Mallards

banked over the northeast corner of the lake,
threw back their wings
and came down in a line-crowded splash
you could hear.
You saw the splash alight
in the black water under an overcast dusk.
An occasional squawk kept the dark friendly.

They Woke Me on a Winter Morning

The light was white. The sky white. Air a wide hollow of evening cold.
From my window I could see the hillside and wind-louvered snow.
My daughter's hand on my forehead like a draft in the room

had entered my sleep and brought me back to see.
Five deer on a green patch below white cedars faced the house.
Their cocked ears, conches left on the shore to bleach in the sun.
Their eyes wide as black walnuts.

When the deer stepped forward a little uphill toward us,
they could have been trying to see our faces and our intentions.
Brown fur folded over in the wind along their backs
like a dark sea washing in in the morning.

The deer listened for any direction to set their day.
Their thin legs didn't show weakness. Sharp lines and angles
showed shaped control for trigger execution
and curves that could spring into buckshot runs.

They stood heavy bottomed, but their heads were focused
like ship prows trained in a sea of snow. Eyes dark, tense.
If light splintered or sparked too sharply,
if sun broke through, they would be gone.

I saw. I saw the light sharpen a ray of gold and burn shade off the hill.
The room lightened and looked out. Air stood crisp.
I was awake to the world. The deer were gone.

WHAT I SEE
AND REMEMBER

What I See and Remember

If you weren't there to hear,
I'd let it all go.

Think of that fisher you told me about.
It came from under the blue spruce on the side hill
and climbed the bank beyond the window.

I saw it with your telling,
how it carried its long tail
like a running fox. Your blue eyes sparked
like the blue-black fisher as it ran in its shine
up the embankment beyond the frame of our windows.

Solitary Prints

On a dusting of snow fox tracks ahead of us
and a keen absence in the air.

Sometimes you have to find things to say.

There are neighbors haven't come for years.
Then we heard some had moved away.

The one we tried to remember to visit
killed himself one May morning.

Even now we miss them all.

da Vinci's *Lady with Ermine*

Thick snow held
even after days of sun.
Maybe you could feel a turn.
Loving had become playful
as in those early years
when twitters of passing birds
could set things off.

Then we saw a white ermine
running up a tree ... another
running after ... determined
as hummingbirds or a dash
saying *look*—
or *see—beauty is light on snow.*

Probably you remember
how kings have sported white ermine robes,
how Russians still prize great coats
with white ermine collars,
and you've seen da Vinci's young *Lady* ...
holding a large white ermine in her arms.
Maybe the taste of loss hangs over us all.

Flowers Live Awhile

We go on,
the lake under the ice
making low moans,
the ice cover arched, fissures wider.

It's been a warm February,
though today wind is back
and snow showers.

All day we wander in and out,
stand at windows restless
as passing ducks. If we have to leave,
I would like to come back and start over.

Tundra Swans

Maybe that year they stayed too long.
We'd seen them ... and again
when ice opened farther down river.

Our landscape leafless at that time
and the snow white, white ... the river
open and dark in the distance, the swans

so white on the dark river, their long
white necks held line-straight,
bills ink black. Two white swans disappearing

in the black ... When we didn't see them
and heard that some thoughtless boy
shot them, we thought, you know,

about desires and how some things
can be so beautiful
we try to keep them for ourselves.

Running on Snow Crust

the red fox leapt over the world,
a hawk returning.

But night and cold
kept everything silent. Hidden.
He hadn't eaten for days.

At dawn he stood under the red pine
searching the air,
almost remembering.

Morning light buffed his coat
and shined his full tail to its white tip.

Pine Grosbeak

The light on the snow shouted
even through the window.
You had called me, and I had come.

That bird that finally showed at the feeder—
yellow-crowned,
mustard-headed bird in bright light.
That must be love,

I remember thinking. You smiling,
bright-headed bird ending a snow-heavy March.

The Fawn

Today as she rooted and nuzzled
through the first wet layers of snow and leaves
for the greenest clumps of grass,
she held her right back hoof
limp and bent back at the ankle
like a broken wing.

We looked from the window,
as if we were tiptoeing
past a sleeping child's room
and hardly breathing
to not disturb her grazing.

Peepers

They keep peeping
and peeping
these pieces of lichen
come down
from the trees
to the shallows.

They call,
peeping
in the falling light,
in the wind,
and the chill
settling.

From the mouth of the river
a chorus of peepers
calling, peeping
as dusk darkens
and falls,
but for their singing,
holding.
Holding it all.

The Finale

for Christina Vosberg

Every day the cardinal fluttered and pecked,
pecked and fluttered at a window.
Crazy bird, he made us say.

When he clicked at her window,
our daughter awoke, said Chris
had come to say her last *goodbye*.

On our side he sometimes sat in the spruce—
red-scarlet, black face.
Beautiful. Beautiful ... He *Was*.

Crossing Point

When the red fox stopped
at the edge of the woods and stared,
I said, *How's it going?*
and kept walking toward her.

She leapt out of the gravel road and into the woods.

At Iverson's drive, I slowed.
She would be there, waiting at that edge
behind brush or a tree, watching.
I passed and looked back in the gap of a breath.

She was gone. Silence stood.

That Day

when we were leaving for America,
being driven to Genoa and the huge ship,
Uncle Ivo confronted Papà in the cantina
where Nonno made and kept his wine.
The bedroom set belongs to the House, Uncle was saying.

I had walked in from the piazza since the door was open.
Papà never said how he had bought the set.
His eyes were red and wet.

Years later in America we always wondered
about Papà and Uncle Ivo being closer
than either of them was to Uncle Jerry,
but Mamma always said,
Your Papà in his mind never holds on to a thing.

In the Night

You could hear the wind's wind-ups
whap against the house.
Walls creaked with snaps
that must have troubled our sleep.
We turned often,
knocked an arm or foot
against each other,
running from a gnawing ache.

And the lake under its ice lid
moaned for a breath
and here and there rubbed and scratched
trying to poke a finger through.

In the morning we awoke
to the same icy brittle world,
I thought,
before the light broke through,
before noon. The wind continued,
but we walked tree-lined trails
like salmon running rivers.

How a Small Deer

How a small deer splashed
across a shallow river
on a late afternoon,
a sky threatening rain.

I wished you had been there.
Maybe the gray light
tinged the deer's flanks
and belly, so thin,

the deer's leap
was naked and shear.
I knew then my love for you
was a leap out of my skin.

Fishy Words

Once in a while it's good to let a five-pound fish go,
I said as my daughter stepped into the lake.

She eased the fish up to a vertical stance
and released—what to us was a record catch.
My mind smelled waves of heat above the castiron
pan of oil if the fish went belly up again.

Behind the fish, she began fishtailing the fish's tail
to awaken a habit a mouthful made us forget.

And I saw her slide a hand along its back,
like a wish,
a blown kiss,
and the fish was gone.

Birds Come in Bunches

    for Rosemary

Birds come in bunches to feed at feeders,
at suet, at red-berried holly bushes and trees.
Chickadees and yellow-rumped warblers come
and yellow and purple finches. Cardinals, male and female come
not for thistle seeds but for sunflower kernels. Bluebirds
and song sparrows search the ground for tidbits.

Some bluebirds explore the three blue birdhouses,
mostly the females go in to look around
while the males watch from a close-by branch.
Robins and grackles rake the ground, pecking like chickens.

Suddenly one wave from the top left corner of the yard will lift off,
then another, and another like an armful tossed to the right
where the wind waited

and takes them by a wing. It's beautiful how the birds grab on
letting the wind have their featheriness.
Seeing them leave in these waves makes us less lonely.

House Wren

Our brown wren is back,
his twitterings dancing on the wind,
though the scarlet hawthorn sleeps on
in a self-wrap above the birdhouse.

And you should see the little dusky
tuft, busy as a bee. He disappears
and reappears at the clay pot's hole,
letting go billfuls of old grass, twigs, feathers.

But when the sun sparks damp spruce tips
along the hill, his gurgling, bubbling rush
above it all, his washing fall of song
speaks even to the light.

Indigo Bunting

When my words were not enough
and I wished I could play
like Rachmaninoff
and sweep you away,

a small gray-black bird came
to the deck railing,
fluttered at the window,
a gentle flutter,
and sat again along the railing

as the sun rose above the trees.
I saw the bird's deep, deep blue,
the quiet blue and wanted it for you.

Line Tension

Moths leapt at the window.
A mosquito droned around me.
I replay the last cast,
the fish leaping out of its world,
the silver spoon finishing its heavenly arc
arching to meet it, the sudden pull...

the moths settling on the window,
the mosquito droning and droning,
the taut line between my fingers,
the poem let go.

Towhee Along Kelly Lake Road

The black head and black back had a sheen,
but the rufous sides and white underparts remarked that bird.
And the yellow eye with black pupil looking out.

Glancing back, you saw the bird was ducked
in a low clump of hazel brush along Kelly Lake Road,
bent down and ready to spring if you stopped or looked too long.

It was the look of his eye that held the light
and made you remember the late afternoon wind, sun at tree line,
the friend with Parkinson's still undecided, still alive.

Late Snapper

Shepherding the old snapper off the middle of the highway
and down the swale while cars and trucks zoomed past
and a pickup stopped to ask,

Was it dead? We'd take it and sell it?
I said, *No! She's laying eggs*, and waved him on.

On her sculpted shell splotched with green moss,
she carried a curled yellow birch leaf

though it was still mid-July, but she was late
and farther from the lake than it seemed safe.
What could we do but take with us the worry of it all?

Mid-June the Muskrat

Each time she comes back
she finds another good niche
to stack greens in the walls
of her burrow under the birch
hanging over the shore.
He can gather into darkness.

I could watch them for as long ...

Steam rises off the lake flowing west.
Cold wind in a gray afternoon.
The shore and beyond, lush and green.
In the shadow of grass, blueberries fatten.

All Day You Were Gone

I could stretch my arm out
and touch yours as I watch you
finish a slice of buttered toast.

All day the sunny room felt chill.
Now as I watch you slide your index finger
around the edge of the plate and press
down to bring the last crumbs and small
seeds gathered to your lips, I realize
I am warm. A warm scent hangs in the room

after you leave. The new moon,
still large, will climb over the house
and warm the darkened pond into the morning.

Cranes

Brown cranes stand like a man
with a heavy bottom
who is wearing a cap with a long visor.

But they lift off with more ease
than a philosopher's thoughts,
with smooth lapping wings,
hammocks swinging in the wind.

Metaphors straggle behind them—
pesky blackbirds
trying to steal grace from their flight.

Gnats

Stretched uphill onto the small tussock
at the end of the channel opening to Birch Lake,
he looked dead. Only the tip of his tail hung in the water.
His shell was dry. His paws hung dulled.
I nudged him with the tip of my paddle,
and he turned my way with a long
exhausted sniff.

                      A week later we found
the old snapper at the edge of a tuft of reed grass
in an inlet of the smallest island, two hundred
feet from the channel. He must have been coming
there to die and only paused for a breath on that
small tussock. Gnats swarmed around his stench
and followed our heads to the far side of the lake

where our words or their sounds dropped.
Turtles, too, have to die, you said. A small
swarm of gnats was at the back of my head.

Loon Moment

Maybe that moment she saw a glint of light from my eyes.
Maybe my body heat radiated toward her on the slow-moving waves.

She dunked her sharp bill in the water, dove, and came up.
Did a quick look right, left, and dove again,
and came up closer than a hundred feet.

I stopped like a fallen rock in the cooling lake.

She stretched upward and again. Fanned out her wings and shook them.
Beads of water splashed on the lake like rain.

Maybe that moment I tried to think like a pickerel weed that bloomed
after the spikes of the rest have turned brown. That moment I looked at her,
and her red eye looked at me, and she dove.

She was down a long, long time. She came up far ... far.

Come Late

Come late, what could a dark dragonfly do?
She clung to a lower clapboard of the house,
bathing in the sun's lower angle
until her wings and shoulders warmed and dried.
And it felt like a short day
following hunger searches and for cover
hanging to the shadow of leaves.
In late afternoon in a mild, incessant wind,
she fell in open-mouthed with the rest heading windward west,
swallowing the new with bits of old news.

The Hatchlings

Perfect miniatures heading
toward the lake that late August morning.

Summer days had shortened,
turned cool, but this was a start—
snapper hatchlings marching.

Having risen from a dark hole,
they were an unstoppable column of replicas,
heads up, tender necks stretched beyond soft shells,
sand dust and grains of sand clinging to their newness.

Pulled by an odor of green, of water and weeds,
they followed a thirst and a need to fill it.

Walking in the Distance

the red fox glanced back,
stopped, turned, and sat in the middle of the road
looking ...

Stood up, gave a look that took in all ...
then entered the woods.

Acknowledgements

"A Red Fox Again" in *Wisconsin Poets Calendar,* 1987; *New Roads Old Towns* (Rountree Publications, UW-P, 1988); *Wisconsin Poetry* (Wisconsin Academy, UW-EUC, 1991); *Out Harmsen's Way* (Fireweed Press, 1991); *Ancient Moves* (Bur Oak Press, 1998)
"Big Bluestem" in *Ancient Moves* (Bur Oak Press, 1998)
"Da Vinci's *Lady with Ermine*" in *Moss Piglet* (November 2021)
"Running on Snow Crust" in *Moss Piglet* (May 2022)
"Sometimes You Push Back the Curtains," "Where You Were Headed," "You Could Smell the Wind," and "You Saw that Fox Running" in *Tracks on Damp Sand* (North Star Press, 2014).
"Towhee along Kelly Lake Road" in *Moss Piglet* (May 2022)
"Waiting" in *Firstborn* (North Star Press, 2016)
"Where You Were Headed" in *The Christian Science Monitor* (March 5, 2012).

ABOUT THE AUTHOR

Franco Pagnucci, Emeritus Professor of English at the University of Wisconsin-Platteville, has published storytelling books for teachers and students and seven volumes of poetry: *Firstborn* (2016); *Breath of the Onion—Italian-American Anecdotes* (2015); *Tracks on Damp Sand* (2014); a chapbook *Imprints of Your Tires on Damp Sand* (2012); *Ancient Moves* (1998); *I Never Had a Pet* (1992); *Out Harmsen's Way* (1991); as well as two poetry anthologies: *New Roads Old Towns* (1988) and *Face the Poem* (1979). His essays have appeared in such publications as *The Christian Science Monitor* and *Commonweal*. Poems of his have been published in many periodicals and anthologies, including *News of the Universe*, *American Voices*, and the *Best American Poetry, 1999*. He and Susan Pagnucci, a graphic designer and paper artist, live on the east coast of NC, where they work on handmade books.

photo by Susan Pagnucci

www.ingramcontent.com/pod-product-compliance
Lightning Source LLC
Chambersburg PA
CBHW030529080526
44586CB00011B/377